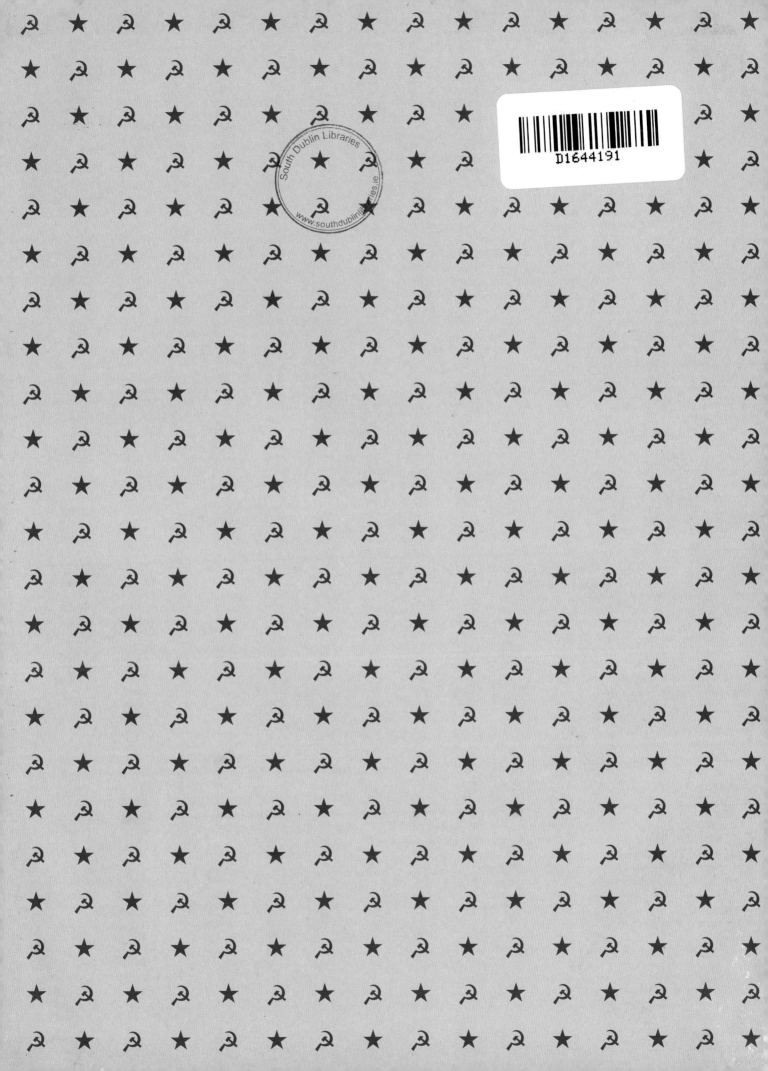

20TH CENTURY RUSSIA

A CENTURY OF UPHEAVAL

HEATHER MAISNER

FRANKLIN WATTS
LONDON • SYDNEY

Franklin Watts

First published in Great Britain in 2016 by The Watts Publishing Group

Editor: Amy Pimperton
Art Director: Peter Scoulding
Designer: John Christopher/White Design
Cover design: Peter Scoulding
Consultant: Geoffrey Hosking
Picture Researcher: Diana Morris
Picture credits:
I Adams/Shutterstock: 58. AP/Topfoto: 56t, 56b. Bain Collection/Library of Congress: 13. Georgia Bateman: 8b, 50b.
S Borisov/Dreamstime: 7t. Karl Karlovich Bulla/cc Wikimedia Commons: 7c. Mary Evans PL/Alamy: 17c. Everett Collection/Alamy: 53t.
Fine Art Images/Superstock: 15b. Fine Art Images/HIP/Topfoto: 19t, 21c, 22t, 24t, 30, 45b, 46, 54bl, 55t. HIP/Alamy: 28, 29b.
HIP/Getty Images: 41. HIP/Topfoto: 37, 38bl. Hulton Archive/Getty Images: 31t. Imagno/Austrian Archives/Topfoto: 27t.
ITAR TASS/Topfoto: 5t, 18, 40, 45t, 52b, 54br, 57. Sergey Kamshylin/Shutterstock: 4b. Jacques Langevin/Sygma/Corbis: 39t.
Oleg Lastochkin/Sputnik/Topfoto: 44. Peter Moeller/Topfoto: 55b. National Archives & Records admin/Wikimedia: 48b.
Nostaligia for Infinity/Shutterstock: 59. Pictorial Press/Alamy: 35bl. Picturepoint/Topfoto: 38br. Print Collector/HIP/Topfoto: 20, 27c.
Ria Novosti/Topfoto: 17t, 22b, 23b, 52t. SCRSS/Topfoto:9t, 25t, 32b. Shutterstock: front cover. Sovfoto/UIG/Getty Images: 34, 47b, 53b.
State Russian Museum St Petersburg/cc Wikimedia Commons: 4-5. Topfoto: 1, 26, 36, 42b. ullsteinbild/Topfoto: 47t, 49t, 49b.
Universal History Archive/Getty Images: 43. Brad Verter/cc Wikimedia Commons: 50. Vladimir Museum/cc Wikimedia Commons: 7b.
WHA/Topfoto: 33. cc Wikimedia Commons: 6t, 8t, 10t, 10b, 11b, 12, 15t, 16, 17b, 25c, 29t, 31b, 32t, 35t, 35br, 39b, 42t, 48t, 51b.
World History Archive/Alamy: 19b. Yekaterinburg State Museum/Superstock: 14. Yui/Shutterstock: 21b.
Every attempt has been made to clear copyright. Should there be any inadvertent omission please apply to the publisher for rectification.

Hardback ISBN 978 1 4451 5034 5
Library eBook ISBN 978 1 4451 5499 2

Printed in China

Franklin Watts
An imprint of
Hachette Children's Group
Part of The Watts Publishing Group
Carmelite House
50 Victoria Embankment
London EC4Y 0DZ

An Hachette UK company.
www.hachette.co.uk
www.franklinwatts.co.uk

For my mother and father, Fanny and Jack – HM

CONTENTS

INTRODUCTION

The greatest event to shape world politics in the 20th century was the Russian Revolution of 1917. For the first time in history, a movement in the name of the working classes took control of government.

Soviet communism was the starting point for many world events in a century of great upheaval. It inspired people to fight for socialism in places as diverse as South America, China, Vietnam, Korea and parts of Africa.

But while many people around the world were attracted to the communist ideal, capitalist governments everywhere — fearing the end of capitalism — tried to stop the spread of communist influence.

IN THEIR OWN WORDS

Workers of the world unite. You have nothing to lose but your chains!
Communist Manifesto, 1848
Karl Marx and
Friedrich Engels

★ **SOVIET FLAG**
This flag became a symbol of communism throughout the world. The hammer and sickle represent workers and peasants, and the red star the rule of the Communist Party.

PRE-REVOLUTIONARY RUSSIA

At the turn of the 20th century, 130 million people lived in Russia, the largest country in the world. The majority were Russian (Slav), but there were over twenty other nationalities, including Ukrainians, Poles, Latvians and many others – all governed by Russia's ruler, the tsar.

Eighty per cent of the population lived west of the Ural Mountains, where the main cities of Moscow and St Petersburg lie. The harsh climate to the east makes farming difficult and in the Arctic tundra, little survives in temperatures that can fall to -70°C.

Four-fifths of the population were peasants and until 1861 most were serfs – bound to the land of their birth, serving the landowners or the State. Sometimes people were treated little better than animals, yoked together to pull barges along the river. When the crops failed due to bad climate or management, many died of illness and starvation. Serfdom was officially abolished in 1861. The intelligentsia hoped this would make life better for the peasants, but for most people life remained much the same.

Nevertheless, Russia was beginning to industrialise. Factories were growing up in the towns and cities, and the trans-Siberian railway, the most ambitious engineering project of the age, ran from one end of Russia to the other.

★ **TRANS-SIBERIAN RAILWAY**
The trans-Siberian railway, begun in 1891, covered 8,000 km and nine time zones.

★ **THE BARGE HAULERS**
Barge Haulers on the Volga,
Ilya Repin, 1873.

A DIVIDED SOCIETY

The aristocracy lived lives of luxury in opulent palaces and mansions, with up to 500 servants. Their sons were privately educated by tutors, then sent abroad to study. Their daughters were sent to boarding schools, where they learned to play musical instruments and speak several languages.

For the workers in the towns, life was hard. A 1904 survey revealed that workers lived in crowded conditions, with roughly six to a room, or slept on wooden planks in factories beside their machines.

THE TSAR

Nicholas II came to power in 1894 at the age of 26. The last tsar of the Romanov Dynasty, which had ruled Russia for over 300 years, he was naturally shy and unwilling to rule the largest empire in the world. But he believed he had been chosen by God to do so, and promised: ' ... *in devoting all my strength on behalf of the people, I shall defend the principle of autocracy as unswervingly as my dead father.*'

Anyone who questioned his power was treated as a traitor. They could be arrested and imprisoned, sent to Siberia or forced to do hard labour in the frozen wastelands of eastern Russia.

Nicholas was a weak tsar, greatly influenced by his German wife, Empress Alexandra. They had four daughters and one son, Alexei, who suffered from life-threatening haemophilia – the failure of blood to clot.

IN THEIR OWN WORDS

My poor Nicky's [Nicholas'] cross is heavy, all the more so as he has nobody on whom he can thoroughly rely.

Empress Alexandra

⭐ **PETERHOF (PETRODVORETS)**

Fountains and golden statues sparkle in the
sunshine at the Grand Palace, outside St Petersburg.

RASPUTIN

Gregory Rasputin was a holy man, who came
to the Russian court in 1907. He was the only
person able to ease Prince Alexei's pain from
internal bleeding and keep him calm.

Empress Alexandra believed Rasputin was sent
to her by God. His enemies called him '*the mad monk*', but to her
he was a '*dear friend*'. He came to have so much influence at court
that he even had a say in the choice of government ministers.
He said of the tsar: '*He's a sad man; he lacks guts*'.

⭐ **RASPUTIN**

Despite the fact he rarely washed,
society women, seen here surrounding a
seated Rasputin, loved his company and
many claimed to have slept with him.

RELIGION

Alongside the tsar, the Russian Orthodox Church was
extremely powerful and had great control over the peasantry.
There were religious rituals for almost every day. Children
were baptised at birth and given a saint's name; saints'
days were as important as birthdays. Most big events in life
received the priest's blessing.

⭐ **ICON**

Icons (religious
images) were kept
at home or carried
around for prayer
and protection
against misfortune.

The State provided money to support the clergy and their
families, and the Church was expected to carry out the tsar's
orders. This included informing on criminals and dissenters,
and passing on information about treason, even when this
came through confessions. An old saying went: '*Nobody can
judge the tsar or the priest.*'

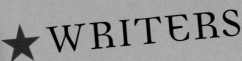
★ WRITERS

Russian writers responded to the political stirrings of the 19th century, creating major plays and works of literature. At this time, there was a huge division in Russian society between the written and spoken word: the gentry preferred speaking French, while the peasants spoke a basic, lively Russian, full of proverbs and slang.

★ CYRILLIC
The Russian language uses the Cyrillic script, which is based largely on the Greek alphabet.

★ ANNA KARENINA
Tolstoy's *Anna Karenina* is considered to be a masterpiece of European literature.

LANGUAGE
Some nobles' children were forbidden to speak Russian in polite society. At one of the best girls' schools in Moscow, pupils who spoke in Russian were made to wear a red tin bell all day and stand in the corner. Most nobles spoke French as well as they did Russian.

In the 18th and 19th centuries, writers and poets began to write in their native language and many are now considered among the greatest writers of Europe:

ALEXANDER PUSHKIN
Pushkin — one of Russia's most influential and renowned writers — was exiled for creating satirical pieces against the Russian government. He is best known for his 'novel in verse' *Eugene Onegin*, about the life of a young dandy in St Petersburg.

Other great writers include Nikolai Gogol, Ivan Turgenev, Fyodor Dostoevsky, Anton Chekhov and Leo Tolstoy.

LEO [LEV] TOLSTOY
Tolstoy was a soldier, landowner, philosopher and writer, who chose to dress like a peasant. He began to write when serving as an artillery officer. He was a commander in the Crimean War before settling at his family's huge estate, Yasnaya Polyana, where he opened a school for peasants.

TOLSTOY'S EPIC NOVELS

The huge sweeping panoramas of Tolstoy's novels encapsulate both the personal and social upheavals of Russian society. His major works, *Anna Karenina* and *War and Peace*, reveal a complex world of rich and poor, men and women, gentry and peasants, in the countryside and the salons of St Petersburg and Moscow, against the backdrop of war and peace.

In his later years, Tolstoy turned his back on European fiction, including his own. He condemned the State and the Church and spread his own code of beliefs based on non-resistance to evil, dedicating himself to the ideal 'simple peasant' life.

He was excommunicated by the Orthodox Church and his funeral was the first non-religious funeral of an aristocrat in Russia. Yet he had the reputation almost of a saint due to his philosophy of peaceful, non-aggression.

★ THE CHERRY ORCHARD

Russian director Konstantin Stanislavski's 1904 production of playwright Anton Chekhov's *The Cherry Orchard* captured the unease of the middle classes at this time.

STIRRINGS OF REVOLUTION

The *Communist Manifesto* begins, '*A spectre is haunting Europe ...*' – the spectre of working-class revolt.

Karl Marx believed that the struggles between different social classes shaped history and that the proletariat (workers) would eventually rise up against their masters. In the ideal, classless communist state, all people would be equal and everyone would work for the good of the community. It would be:

'*From each according to his abilities, to each according to his needs ...*'

★ **KARL MARX**

Karl Marx (1818–83), one of the most influential thinkers of all time, wrote the *Communist Manifesto* with Friedrich Engels. Marx's most famous major work is *Das Capital*.

KARL MARX

Marx's theory, known as Marxism, claims that modern societies produce class struggles between owners who control production, and workers who provide the labour for production. He believed that the workers would eventually destroy the capitalist owners and a new socialist society would emerge.

Marxism was very popular with the intelligentsia in Europe at the turn of the 20th century, when industrialisation was creating a poor urban class of workers. Marxist interpretation of history depended on an industrialised country with a large urban working class. Many believed that Russia, with its huge peasant population and small working class, was only just reaching the capitalist stage in its development and was not yet ready for revolution.

BLOODY SUNDAY

In 1904, Russia went to war with Japan and experienced many unexpected losses. At home, there were disturbances and strikes.

On Sunday 22 January 1905, an Orthodox priest called Father Gapon led a group of about 200,000 workers in a peaceful protest to the Winter Palace in St Petersburg to present a petition to the tsar. The crowd carried icons of '*their Father Tsar*' and believed he would sympathise with their demands for: amnesty for political prisoners, full civil liberties, better working conditions and an end to war.

But the tsar had left the capital, leaving orders to prevent any disturbances. The palace guards panicked and fired on the crowd, killing and wounding hundreds of people.

Across the country, people responded with strikes and assassinations. In June, troops dispersed crowds in Odessa, killing thousands of civilians after the crew of the *Battleship Potemkin* mutinied and tried to land.

In the continuing unrest peasants turned against landowners, destroying around 3,000 manors. Eventually, in 1906, the tsar agreed to set up a Duma – elected parliament. However, he could dissolve it at any time.

IN THEIR OWN WORDS

Sire, we workers ... have come to seek from you, truth and protection ... We are impoverished and oppressed, unbearable work is imposed on us, we are despised and not recognised as human beings. We are treated as slaves and we have suffered terrible things ...
Workers' Petition, January 1905

★ BATTLESHIP POTEMKIN

The crew of the *Battleship Potemkin* mutinied at sea and then tried to land at the port of Odessa.

★ BLOODY SUNDAY

Bloody Sunday in St Petersburg, Wojciech Horacy Kossak, 1905. The peaceful protest outside the Winter Palace, led by Father Gapon carrying a crucifix, soon turned deadly.

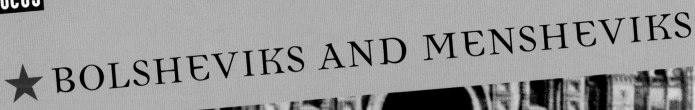

★ BOLSHEVIKS AND MENSHEVIKS

★ LENIN
Vladimir Lenin addresses a crowd in Red Square, Moscow, after the October Revolution in 1917.

IN THEIR OWN WORDS

The masses must be made to see that the Soviet Workers' Deputies are the only possible form of revolutionary government ...

Lenin,
April 1913

The political landscape was changing slowly, but the thinking of revolutionaries was moving faster. Vladimir Lenin, one of the most controversial and influential leaders of the 20th century, played a major role in the acceleration of change.

LENIN

Lenin was born Vladimir Ilyich Ulyanov in 1870 in the town of Simbirsk. When he was 17, his elder brother was hanged for conspiracy after an assassination attempt on Tsar Alexander III. Lenin was determined to avoid the same fate. He studied law at Kazan University, but was expelled for taking part in a student demonstration. In 1889 he declared himself a Marxist and in 1895 he was arrested and exiled to Siberia for three years, where he changed his name to Lenin.

SOCIAL DEMOCRATIC LABOUR PARTY

In 1898, the Social Democratic Labour Party was founded, inspired by the teachings of Karl Marx. Party members (including Lenin) believed that the tsar would be deposed by an uprising of the proletariat, but they disagreed about how revolution should come about. In 1903 the party split into two groups: the Bolsheviks and the Mensheviks

THE SPLIT

The Bolsheviks believed that a true Socialist Revolution had to be made by the workers, but that they needed to be led by a small group of full-time revolutionaries. They wanted all party members to be activists. Lenin became leader of the Bolsheviks, which means 'men of the majority' because at an important meeting his faction won by a small majority.

The Mensheviks, meaning 'men of the minority', believed the revolutionary party should be a mass party containing many workers and that, until industry was far more developed, the workers' party should ally itself with the reformist bourgeoisie – middle classes – a class of people whom Lenin distrusted.

TROTSKY

Leon Trotsky, born Lev Davidovich Bronstein in 1879 in Yanovka, Ukraine, helped set up the Southern Russian Workers' Union. Aged 19, he was arrested and sent to Siberia for four years. He escaped and went to London, where he changed his name to Trotsky.

In 1903 he became a Menshevik and returned to Russia to support the uprisings that followed Bloody Sunday. In 1906 he was sent to Siberia again, but escaped two years later. He spent the next years in exile, denouncing the First World War (1914–18) and urging workers not to fight. In 1917 he joined the Bolsheviks.

SOCIALIST REVOLUTIONARY PARTY

Formed in 1901, another political party (known as the SRs) also aimed to rid the country of the tsar. But the party was divided between those who believed in mass terror and carried out over 2,000 assassinations, and those who wanted to work for radical but peaceful reform to give land to the peasants 'who worked it'. Alexander Kerensky was a leading SR member.

IN THEIR OWN WORDS

The moment has come when ... we must stretch out the hand of brotherhood to the proletarians of all countries and proclaim forcefully and loudly: We do not want war! Long live peace!
Petrograd Mensheviks, 1917

★ **TROTSKY**
Trotsky became a great military leader, recruiting over five million soldiers into the Red Army.

★ ARTISTS IN THIS ERA

The first two decades of the 20th century were an exciting and energetic period of artistic change and innovation all over Europe, especially in Russia. The Symbolist and Futurist movements began, followed by Suprematism and Constructivism.

POETRY

Futurist poet Vladimir Mayakovsky was eager to create a new language for poetry, free from the usual emotional content. He wanted to end everyday routines, sweep away the clutter of the past and replace petty bourgeois life with a new, spiritual existence. He believed a new culture could be built on the destruction of the old, stating: *'It's time for bullets to pepper museums.'*

PAINTING

Russian modernist painters — Leon Bakst, Vasili Kandinsky and Marc Chagall were among Europe's most influential artists of the early 20th century.

In 1915, Kazimir Malevich launched Suprematism, an art movement devoted to the purity of geometric form, using circles, crosses and triangles.

In 1919, Vladimir Tatlin launched Constructivism, creating structures made of glass, metal and wire, in celebration of a new socialist industrial society.

★ MALEVICH

Malevich used overlapping geometric shapes in different sizes and colours to create the illusion of movement in space, as in this painting from 1915.

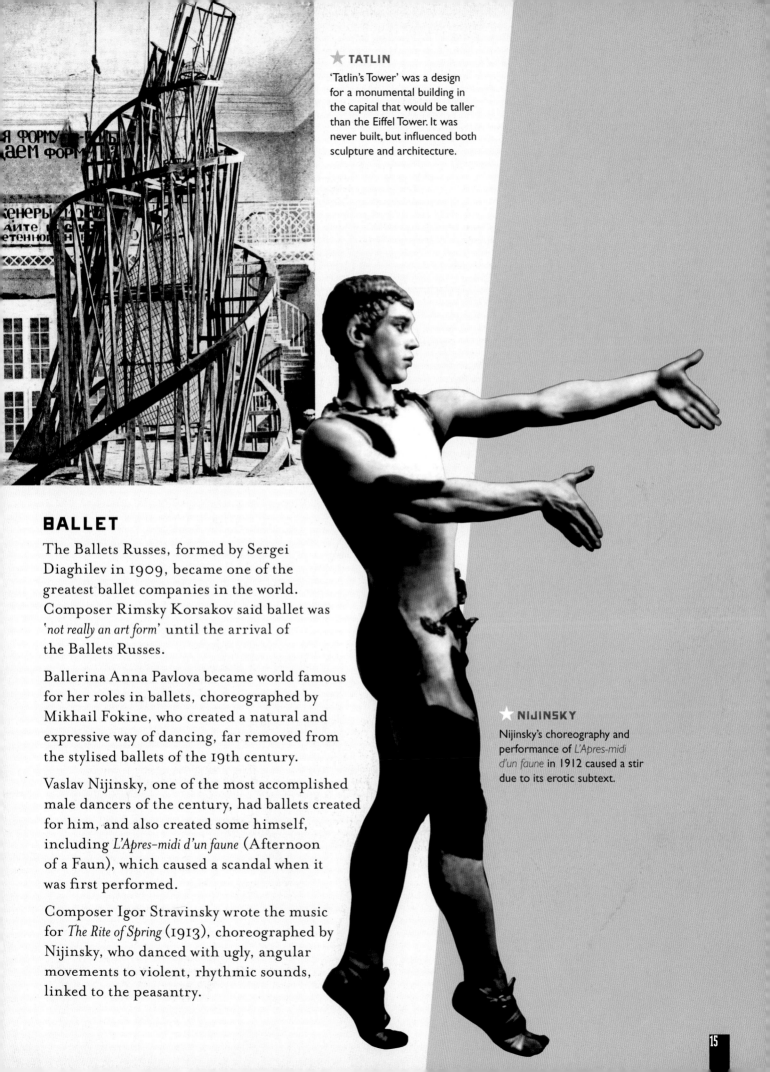

★ TATLIN

'Tatlin's Tower' was a design for a monumental building in the capital that would be taller than the Eiffel Tower. It was never built, but influenced both sculpture and architecture.

BALLET

The Ballets Russes, formed by Sergei Diaghilev in 1909, became one of the greatest ballet companies in the world. Composer Rimsky Korsakov said ballet was *'not really an art form'* until the arrival of the Ballets Russes.

Ballerina Anna Pavlova became world famous for her roles in ballets, choreographed by Mikhail Fokine, who created a natural and expressive way of dancing, far removed from the stylised ballets of the 19th century.

Vaslav Nijinsky, one of the most accomplished male dancers of the century, had ballets created for him, and also created some himself, including *L'Apres-midi d'un faune* (Afternoon of a Faun), which caused a scandal when it was first performed.

Composer Igor Stravinsky wrote the music for *The Rite of Spring* (1913), choreographed by Nijinsky, who danced with ugly, angular movements to violent, rhythmic sounds, linked to the peasantry.

★ NIJINSKY

Nijinsky's choreography and performance of *L'Apres-midi d'un faune* in 1912 caused a stir due to its erotic subtext.

THE FIRST WORLD WAR

In August 1914, Russia declared war on Germany and Austria–Hungary, and became part of the First World War. At first the war was popular in Russia, bringing different political and social groups together to defend the country. However, the war went on longer than expected and the Russian army was very short of supplies: one million men didn't always have rifles or proper clothing. Soldiers were poorly trained and there were few strong commanders.

★ **TRAIN AND PEASANTS**
Across the country, hungry peasants crowded up to trains, looking for food.

IN THEIR OWN WORDS

… day after day, since I entered military service, I have been cursing the day I was born. … As soon as I arrived in the unit, they tried to beat all human feeling out of me, every superior scolds and punishes me without sorting out whether I am right or not, but just because he has a right to …

Anonymous soldier, December 1913

FOOD SHORTAGES

In the countryside, the requisitioning of horses and fertilisers for the war made it difficult for the peasants to produce enough food. The government didn't want to pay a reasonable price, so farmers and peasants began to hoard stocks.

The army took over the roads and trains, sending supplies to the Front and preventing food from reaching the cities. Refugees from the countryside flooded into the towns and, in the capital – renamed Petrograd to make it sound less German – there was so little grain that bread rationing was introduced, and hunger almost turned to famine.

★ **SOLDIERS**

Soldiers fought in icy conditions; many lacked boots or proper equipment.

WAR LOAN POSTER ★

This War Loan poster was designed to encourage people to '*help our glorious soldiers*'.

The trans-Siberian railway did not function well during the war. By 1916 over 575 stations could no longer handle heavy goods and the lines became blocked. Guns and shells took too long to arrive and the supplies that did arrive piled up. At other depots, food rotted in trucks, unable to move along blocked lines.

Tsar Nicholas went to the Front in an attempt to raise the morale of the soldiers but General Brusilov noted:

'*Although the word "Tsar" still had magical power over the troops, he utterly lacked the charisma to bring that magic to life.*'

RUMOURS

While the tsar was at the Front, rumours circulated that his German wife, Empress Alexandra, who was disliked because the country was at war with Germany, was giving military secrets to the enemy and holding back supplies. Many believed she had too much control over her husband, and now they felt that Rasputin had too much control over her.

Aristocrats, including members of the royal family, begged Alexandra to dismiss Rasputin but she refused. In December 1916, he was murdered after a lengthy attack, in which he repeatedly refused to die – first with poison, then with two bullets shot at point-blank range. Finally, he was battered over the head and drowned in the icy waters of the Fontanka Canal.

★ **RASPUTIN POSTER**

Rasputin holds the tsar and empress in his hands.

REVOLUTION

On 23 February 1917 — International Women's Day — while soldiers fought at the Front in the First World War, women marched through the Russian capital Petrograd, chanting for equality and an end to war. The sound of their voices drew factory and textile workers out to join them.

★ PROTESTS
Women demand the right to vote and an end to war as they march through Petrograd.

FEBRUARY 1917

Over the next few days over 200,000 people marched through the city. Shopkeepers, bankers, students, well-dressed women and children joined the crowd like 'an enormous circus'. The feeling was one of 'rather precarious excitement', wrote British journalist, Arthur Ransome, in the Daily News.

The crowd wore red armbands and red ribbons, waved red flags and banners, shouted 'Down with the Tsar!', yet moved together in 'almost uncanny orderliness and good nature', said The Times. Protesters were given meals in people's homes, and cafes and restaurants gave away food.

The crowd began to persuade soldiers to join them, calling to them as workers and comrades. Bolshevik worker-activist Ilia Mitrofanovich Gordienko recalled:

'Women ... surrounded the Cossacks with a dense human chain. "Our husbands, fathers, brothers are at the Front!" they shouted. "Here we face starvation, an inordinate workload, insults, humiliation, abuses ... You also have mothers, wives, sisters and children; we demand bread and an end to the war!"'

Even some Cossacks, traditionally loyal to the tsar, were persuaded to join the crowd.

TENSIONS BUILD

Petrograd became tense with frustration as, each day, the crowd of demonstrators grew, but ministers played down the situation in their daily reports to the tsar at the Front. Empress Alexandra dismissed what was happening in the city in letters to her husband: *'This is a hooligan movement, young boys and girls running about and screaming ... only to excite — and then workmen preventing others from work ... But this will all pass and calm down ...'*

She urged Nicholas to act and show his authority:

'...I find that anti-dynastic [speeches] ought to be at once very severely punished and as this is a time of war, even more so.'

Nicholas responded by sending a telegram to his general in Petrograd, demanding action that in hindsight was disastrous for his reign: *'I command you tomorrow to stop the disorders in the capital, which are unacceptable in this difficult time of war with Germany and Austria.'*

★ **COSSACKS**

Cossacks, Ivan Alekseevich Vladimirov, 1910s. Cossacks were fierce warriors who traditionally acted as an elite regiment to the tsars.

★ **INSPECTING THE TROOPS**

This painting by Pavel Ryzhenko, 1916, shows Tsar Nicholas II at the Front with his troops.

Troops fired on the crowd and the bloodshed in the streets continued through the following months, as seen in this photo of July 1917.

IN THEIR OWN WORDS

> Our fathers, mothers, sisters, brothers and brides are begging for bread. Are we going to kill them? Did you see the blood on the streets today? I say we shouldn't take up positions tomorrow. I myself refuse to go. And, as one, the soldiers cried out, "We shall stay with you".
>
> Sergeant Sergei Kirpichnikov, February 1917

THE TROOPS RESPOND

The next day, the military obeyed the tsar's orders by sending troops out to fire at the protesters. Soon the streets were covered in blood, but many of the soldiers were horrified at what they had done. When other regiments learned of the massacre they decided to mutiny, shooting officers and Cossacks loyal to the tsar, rather than shooting at the crowd.

Sergeant Sergei Kirpichnikov roused soldiers to change sides, while political activists made the following appeal:

'*COMRADE SOLDIERS! … A soldier's lot is hard. A dog is not treated with less honour … Don't stain your hands with your brothers' blood … If you are ordered to shoot at the people, shoot at those who are giving you orders … Long live the unity of the army and the people! Down with autocracy! Down with war! Long live the revolution! All land to the peasants! All freedom to the people!*'

Workers and soldiers broke into military arsenals and stole over 200,000 rifles, revolvers and guns. They drove cars and lorries wildly through the streets, waving red flags and shooting into the air. Many vehicles, driven by people who had never driven before or were drunk, crashed and were left by the roadside.

LOOTING BEGINS

The crowd set police stations on fire, freeing about 8,000 convicts and prisoners. They raised the red flag above the Peter and Paul Fortress, where political prisoners were held. Then they began to riot. Many wealthy people were mugged in the streets, and houses, shops and warehouses were broken into and burgled.

Nikolai Sukhanov of the Petrograd Soviet recorded:

'... The criminals released with the political prisoners ... were leading the rioters, pillaging and burning. It was not altogether safe in the streets: police, house-porters, Secret Police, and gendarmes were firing from the attics. They were an incitement to rioting and anarchy. A few fires were burning ...'

Writer Maxim Gorky wrote: '... Looting has started. What will happen? I don't know ... Much blood will be spilled, much more than has ever been spilled before.'

THE END OF THE MONARCHY

A deputation of ministers set off to find Tsar Nicholas, who was stranded in a train shunted into a siding by mutinous soldiers and railway workers. In the green lounge of his dining car, ministers told him he had no choice but to abdicate.

Yuri Danilov, general quartermaster of Headquarters for the Supreme Commander, recalled:

'The Tsar went to the desk and several times, apparently without realising it, looked out the carriage window, which was covered with a curtain. His usually expressionless face became unconsciously distorted by a movement of his lips to the side ... It was clear that a certain very burdensome decision was ripening in his soul! ...

Suddenly Emperor Nicholas abruptly turned back to us and pronounced with a firm voice:

"I have made a decision. I have decided to abdicate the Throne...".'

★ **TSAR NICHOLAS II**

Tsar Nicholas was stranded in a train that was shunted into a siding by rebellious railway workers.

Nicholas abdicated in favour of his brother Grand Duke Mikhail, but Mikhail declined to take the throne.

And so ended one thousand years of monarchy in the largest country in the world.

★ **IMPERIAL EAGLE**

The Imperial double-headed eagle – a symbol of the Russian Empire – was torn down from public buildings.

THE OCTOBER REVOLUTION

Following the tsar's abdication, an assembly of political parties formed the Provisional Government, which was soon led by Alexander Kerensky of the SR Party. The government then set about changing the way the country was run.

The tsarist police and the security police were dissolved, and authority was removed from officers in the army, apart from during combat. Citizens were given a full range of civil rights, and the Soviets in town and country were given new powers of control. However, it was decided to continue the war until peace could be negotiated.

Across the country, the changes caused chaos. Workers and Soviets took control of the factories. Rebellious soldiers deserted and ran wild in armed gangs, burning manor houses. Others went back to their villages to help the peasantry seize land from the landowners.

★ KERENSKY

Kerensky of the SR Party and leader of the Provisional Government sits in his office in the Winter Palace, Petrograd.

ATTEMPTED COUP

To restore order, Kerensky appointed General Lev Kornilov as commander-in-chief of the armed forces. Soon he feared that Kornilov wanted to seize power for himself, and he tried to dismiss him. Kornilov refused to stand down and, instead, decided to attack Petrograd. To hold back Kornilov's troops, Kerensky called on the Red Guards to take up arms. Armed Bolsheviks persuaded many of General Kornilov's troops to desert, while railway workers prevented others from entering the city. The coup failed.

Many army officers felt Kerensky had betrayed them. Meanwhile, more and more workers joined the Bolsheviks, who could now claim to be leaders in '*the victory over counter-revolution*'.

From exile in Finland, Lenin denounced the Provisional Government and promoted the idea of a Soviet government, ruled by soldiers, peasants and workers. He urged the Bolsheviks to prepare for the overthrow of Kerensky's government, stating:

DISGUISE ★

Lenin in disguise – clean-shaven and wearing a wig and cap – in October 1917.

'*History will not forgive us if we do not assume power.*'

LENIN RETURNS

Lenin returned to Petrograd in October in disguise, wearing a wig and cap, fearful of arrest. Rumours of a Bolshevik coup were circulating in the city and the government had closed down the Bolshevik newspapers *Pravda* (Truth) and *Izvestia* (News), and ordered the arrest of Bolshevik leaders. Realising the need to act quickly, Lenin ordered the insurrection to begin.

Trotsky, who had returned to Russia in May 1917, had joined the Bolsheviks as leader of the Petrograd Soviet. He now organised the Red Guards to seize key areas of Petrograd, including the bridges and telegraph offices.

OCTOBER 25 1917

The '*storming of the Winter Palace*' on October 25, which later became known as The Great October Socialist Revolution or Red October, in fact took place quite easily. The enormous building of the Winter Palace, which housed the Provisional Government, was guarded by a small group of Cossacks, cadets and Amazons (women fighters). The Red Guards moved in and quickly persuaded them to surrender.

Most of the Provisional Government escaped, including Kerensky, who, like the tsar before him, was at the Front attempting to enlist the help of loyal troops to put down the coup.

From across the River Neva, the sound of guns rang out as the cruiser *Aurora* fired into the air in a pre-arranged signal, telling the people that the Bolsheviks had taken control. Thousands flooded into the palace to celebrate. And so the communist era began.

★ **THE WINTER PALACE**
Storming of the Winter Palace,
Yefim Dyshalyt c. 1917

★ WOMEN IN THE REVOLUTION

КОРМИТЕ
ДѢТЕЙ
ЗАЩИТНИКОВЪ
РОДИНЫ

ПРИБАВКУ ПАЙКА
СЕМЬЯМЪ СОЛДАТЪ
ЗАЩИТНИКАМЪ СВОБОДЫ
и НАРОДНОГО МІРА.

БРАТЬЯ МОРИ

PROTESTORS ★

Women, marching through Petrograd in 1917, calling for freedom and an end to war, lead the path to revolution.

For women of all classes, the year 1917 brought many changes. Before the Revolution women of the gentry, although lacking political power, ran the salons in the major cities and were recognised for their strength of character and witty conversation. Novelist Ivan Turgenev noted that Russian women were stronger in character, temper and decision-making than their men.

PEASANT HOUSEHOLDS

In peasant households life was very different. New brides, living in the extended family homes of their husbands, were treated like servants. They had to accept the sexual advances of a father-in-law, as well as a husband, and often the landowner, too. Wife-beating was common as indicated in this popular saying:

'*The more you beat the old woman, the tastier the soup will be.*'

But at the turn of the century, women were beginning to attend people's universities – voluntary institutions; and women were strong in the revolutionary movement, some serving life sentences for political murders.

In the 1917 February Revolution, it was the women who led the way, urging workers, soldiers and Cossacks to join in the protests on International Women's Day.

FIGHTING FOR CHANGE

After the February Revolution, the Women's Battalion of Death – the Amazons – was formed by Sergeant Maria Bochkarova. With their heads shaven to military length, they were promoted as the fighting spirit of the Russian people.

ALEXANDRA KOLLONTAI

Alexandra Kollontai, daughter of a Cossack general, was a feminist and party agitator. She believed that marriage and the traditional family were part of an oppressive society based on property-rights. Under communism, the family would wither away, people would work for society, and their children would be brought up by society.

PROGRESS

Following the October Revolution, decrees gave women the right to full political involvement at the workplace and 16 weeks maternity leave. Civil marriage became the only legal marriage; women were allowed to keep their maiden names and had equal rights with husbands. The idea of illegitimacy was abolished. Day care centres and public cafes were planned to free women from domestic work.

★ AMAZONS
The Provisional Government used women fighters, heads shaven and dressed like men, to shame deserters and lead men into battle.

★ KOLLONTAI
Kollontai founded the 'Women's Department' of the Soviet Union to fight illiteracy and teach women about the new marriage, education and working laws.

IN THEIR OWN WORDS

In place of indissoluble marriage based on the servitude of women, we shall see rise a free union, fortified by the love and mutual respect of two members of the Workers' State, equal in their rights and obligations.
Alexandra Kollontai, 1918

CREATION OF THE SOVIET UNION

Once in power, the Bolsheviks' immediate needs were to turn an enormous, backward, peasant nation into a modern, industrialised state, and to defend Russia from external forces.

Private ownership was abolished and village committees were given the task of distributing land. Property in towns was handed to the Soviets; the poor were re-housed in the homes of the rich. Workers' Management Boards took control of commercial properties.

CHANGES

Ranks in the army were abolished and soldiers' committees elected to take charge. Law courts were replaced by 'people's courts', with judges elected by workers. The Red Army was founded and the Cheka – security police – was created.

Non-Russian peoples were given their own autonomous republics. Foreign debts were cancelled, railways and banks nationalised, and all schools brought under State control. All titles were abolished and people now greeted one another as 'Comrade'.

Marx called religion 'the opium of the masses'. After the Revolution, religious education was forbidden and the land and property of the Russian Orthodox Church was seized by the State, without compensation. Divine service alone was permitted once a week.

★ A SOLEMN PROMISE

This poster for recruiting people into the Red Army carries the text of the solemn oath taken by Red Army volunteers.

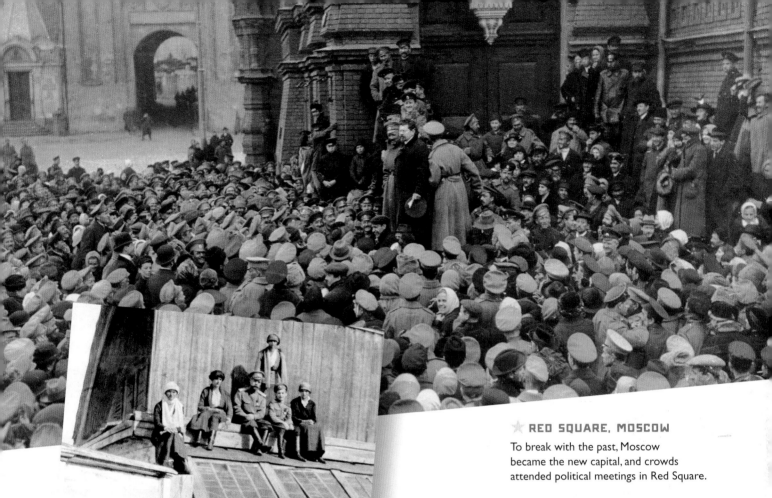

To break with the past, Moscow became the new capital, and crowds attended political meetings in Red Square.

★ MURDER

Tsar Nicholas and his family pose on a roof in Yekaterinburg, shortly before they were murdered.

HOUSE ARREST

To prevent people calling for the return of the tsar, Nicholas and his family were first placed under house arrest and then murdered in 1918. Rumours spread that Princess Anastasia had escaped and, for years, stories circulated about her reappearance in various parts of the world.

PEACE – AT ANY COST

The Bolsheviks hoped that their revolution would be followed by similar European uprisings. But the Russian economy was in a state of collapse and people were exhausted from years of war. Despite disagreement among his supporters, Lenin decided that peace had to be agreed, at any cost. Not everyone agreed with him and tensions in the country increased.

It was a period of enormous and abrupt change, in which Lenin was 'turning Russia upside down, the way I hang my paintings', said artist Marc Chagall.

IN THEIR OWN WORDS

Our impulse tells us to refuse to sign this robber peace ... Russia can offer no physical resistance because she is materially exhausted by three years of war ... the Russian Revolution must sign the peace to obtain a breathing space to recuperate for the struggle.

Lenin, March 1918, on the Treaty of Brest-Litovsk

CIVIL WAR, RED TERROR

★ STARVING WORKERS

Dressing the Dead Horse, Ivan Vladimirov, 1919.
Animals were eaten; even the flesh of human
corpses was sold, as people struggled to survive.

In the chaotic period after the Revolution, thousands of workers returned to their villages, and a lack of food supplies caused near starvation.

Some tsarist generals, admirals and members of other political parties, known as the Whites, decided to attack the Bolsheviks – the Reds – in a Civil War. Russia's old allies, Britain and France, angry with the Bolsheviks for taking Russia out of the First World War, sent money and troops to aid the Whites in what became a three-year Civil War (1918–21).

IN THEIR OWN WORDS

Famine in Petrograd has begun. Almost daily they pick up people who have dropped from exhaustion right in the streets.
Maxim Gorky, 1918

RED ARMY

Threatened from inside and outside the country, the Bolsheviks needed to build a strong army of workers and peasants. However, the Red Army totally lacked military experience. Trotsky, as Commissar for War, invited former tsarist officers to help. General Brusilov appealed to colleagues:

'It is now your duty to defend our beloved Russia with all your strength. [Otherwise] Our descendants will say we have forgotten our own Russian people …'

However, all specialists were supervised by Bolsheviks; any traitors would be shot.

WAR COMMUNISM

To ensure the loyalty of all citizens, the government adopted a policy of War Communism – nationalisation of industry and agriculture, with central control of resources.

From now on, all grain belonged to the State and a set quota was demanded from every villager. Teams of workers were sent to the villages to buy grain or take it by force. If a peasant refused, he could be beaten and arrested, his home searched and furniture destroyed. Rich peasants, known as *kulaks*, were often evicted from their homes. Peasants on the way to market were robbed at armed roadblocks and train stations.

Farmers hid food, and a black market began with the growth of 'bagmen' – peasants carrying sacks of produce. They charged huge prices in makeshift street markets. Or they exchanged food for clothing and other items, such as tools stolen from factories.

THE CHEKA

The Cheka were given powers to execute suspected 'enemies of the State'. These could be the bourgeoisie, peasants hoarding crops or workers who complained. Thousands are believed to have been killed during the conflict.

A new class of privileged and elite officials, the *nomenklatura*, were soon running the Party, holding information on the political reliability of people in key positions, such as factory directors, government officials, head teachers and newspaper editors.

The Civil War was won by the Reds, but it divided families and social groups, and left the country in ruins.

★ **RED CAVALRY**
Red Cavalry, 1932, by Kasimir Malevich portrays the speed and power of the Red Army.

★ **CHEKA**
In Search of the Escaped Kulak, Ivan Vladimirov, 1920.

THE SOVIET UNION

When the Civil War ended in 1921, the Bolshevik Party became the Communist Party and the Soviet Union (USSR – Union of Soviet Socialist Republics) was set up, with Lenin as leader.

NEW ECONOMIC POLICY [NEP]

To revive the economy and bring the cities back to life, Lenin realised a more lenient approach was needed, and the New Economic Policy was introduced.

Farmers were allowed to increase food production and sell it on the open market, paying a small tax to the State. Peasants could rent land and hire workers. Rationing was abolished and small-scale businesses were allowed to function again.

Almost immediately, the country changed. A State Bank was opened and a new rouble coin, which contained gold, replaced paper money. However, some Bolsheviks feared that the return of money would mean a return of capitalism with the old divisions between the rich and the poor.

★ SHOPS

From 1921, small-scale businesses, like this Jewish hat shop, began to function again.

★ SMOLENSK MARKET, MOSCOW

The NEP encouraged farmers to produce more food, and street markets thrived.

IN THEIR OWN WORDS

Shops and stores sprang up overnight, mysteriously stacked with delicacies Russia had not seen for years. Large quantities of butter, cheese and meat displayed for sale ... [People] with pinched faces and hungry eyes stood about gazing into the windows ...

Emma Goldman (Foreign Visitor), 1925, Memoir

NEPMEN

Within a short time, new business people called NEPmen came on the scene and began to grow rich on private trade. They included kulaks, retailers and small manufacturers. Mocked in Bolshevik cartoons, the NEPmen were depicted with wives and mistresses in fur coats, driving huge cars, smoking cigars and visiting the races, while the rest of the country went hungry.

By taxing grain and exporting food, the government was able to buy in the tools and machines it needed for the country to industrialise. In time, the production of coal, electricity, iron, steel and machine tools began to increase.

★ NEPMAN

A typical Bolshevik cartoon, ridiculing a cigar-smoking NEPman.

★ PROPAGANDA AND POSTERS

Shortly after taking power, the Bolsheviks took control of the printing presses and produced newspapers, leaflets and posters, which they sent to towns and cities all over the country. This propaganda promoted the Bolshevik vision of society, portraying Lenin and the Bolshevik leaders as heroically unifying the country, while the Whites were shown as enemies.

★ PROPAGANDA POSTER

Posters played a strong role in winning over the masses. This one reads: 'No place for priests or kulaks on our collective farm'.

RALLYING THE TROOPS

During the Civil War, Trotsky travelled over 100,000 kilometres, from one Front to another to rally the troops in a special armoured train. He said he needed:

'... good commanders, a few dozen experienced fighters, a dozen or so communists ready to make any sacrifice, boots for the barefooted, a bath-house, an energetic propaganda campaign, food, underwear, tobacco and matches ... The train took care of all of this.'

He increased the army to five million men and his work also helped create the myth of Red October.

AGIT-PROP

Agit-prop trains travelled the country with theatre groups to entertain people in village outposts, persuading them to join the Party. Lenin's slogan 'Peace, land and bread' won over the masses.

Director Vsevolod Meyerhold set up a State School for Stage Direction and began teaching directors how to take revolutionary drama out onto the streets, using pantomime, gymnastics and circus tricks.

★ AGIT-PROP TRAIN

Agit-prop trains travelled the country, persuading people to join the Party.

★ BATTLESHIP POTEMKIN

Eisenstein's film, *Battleship Potemkin*, created as an agit-prop film, captures the drama of pre-revolutionary unrest.

CINEMA

Lenin called cinema '*the most important of all the arts*' — a great propaganda tool in a country that was largely illiterate. Churches and village halls were turned into temporary cinemas, where young audiences, often aged about 10–15, enjoyed the new technology that was so true to life.

EISENSTEIN

Film-maker Sergei Eisenstein filled his films with images of young workers, rising up against the capitalists. He used a new technique of montage — intercutting shots to create unusual contrasts and associations — inspired by what he had witnessed in the 1917 Revolution.

MUSIC

In the early creative years of the 1920s, concerts in factories made use of spoons, washboards, sirens, hooters and whistles to embrace working life. Dmitry Shostakovitch composed symphonies, wrote the music for over thirty films and played the piano to silent films. In the climax of his Second Symphony *To October* (1927), he included the sound of factory whistles.

IN THEIR OWN WORDS

I saw people quite unfit, even poorly built for running, in headlong flight. Watches on chains were jolted out of waistcoat pockets. Cigarette cases flew out of side pockets. And canes. Canes. Canes. ... My legs carried me out of range of the machine guns ...

Sergei Eisenstein, 1917

STALIN AND THE CULT OF PERSONALITY

Lenin died in 1924 and was laid in state in a mausoleum in Moscow's Red Square. After his death, he became an almost god-like figure. Millions of people queued in long lines to look at his embalmed figure. Religion had been banned, but the need for it was great in a country that had always been religious.

★ LENIN'S TOMB

The mausoleum was originally made of wood, then rebuilt in stone in 1925.

IN THEIR OWN WORDS

Almost everybody in the great theatre burst into tears and from all parts came the hysterical wailing of women. Tears were running down the faces of the members of the Presidium. The funeral march of the Revolutionaries was played by a weeping orchestra.

Arthur Ransome, 1924, on Lenin's Death

YOUNG STALIN

Stalin, the son of a boot-maker, was born in Georgia in 1879 and named Joseph Dzhugashvili. In his early life, he trained to become a priest, but he was expelled when he became a Marxist. He joined the Bolshevik Party and changed his name to Stalin, meaning 'Man of Steel'. He was arrested and sent to Siberia eight times, but escaped on seven occasions. In 1917 he became editor of the Bolshevik magazine *Pravda* (Truth).

RISE TO POWER

In the fight for leadership after Lenin's death, Stalin, now General Secretary of the Bolshevik Party, used his position to play off one leader against another. He wanted to strengthen communism at home and modernise Russia, promoting, 'Socialism in One Country'. Trotsky, who was a main contender for the leadership, wanted socialism to be spread through continuous international revolutions. But Stalin's view appealed to a country that was tired of war, and he was able to consolidate his position as leader.

★ STALIN AT THE HELM
Benevolent images of Stalin, steering the USSR into a bright and successful future, appeared everywhere.

THE 'GREAT LEADER'

Stalin used propaganda and amended history during his lifetime to make it seem that only he and Lenin had saved the Soviet Union from its enemies. To highlight his own importance he altered photos to eliminate his enemies, notably Trotsky, whose roles in the Revolution and Civil War were totally discredited.

Stalin's kindly, smiling portrait appeared everywhere — on street corners, in offices and shops. At school, children were taught that Stalin was the 'Great Leader', and plays and poems were written about him. Streets in many cities were given his name and the city of Tsaritsyn was changed to Stalingrad. In Moscow, there were huge parades in his honour. Those who wanted to succeed needed to praise him, and he promised to reward those loyal to him.

★ TROTSKY
Stalin changed history, literally wiping out Trotsky's role in the Revolution, as revealed in these two versions of a photograph of Lenin addressing a crowd in Moscow.

FIVE-YEAR PLANS

Stalin introduced a policy of highly centralised Five-Year Plans. More blast furnaces, tractors, tanks, hydroelectric dams and longer railroad tracks were needed. Unless the USSR industrialised quickly, it could be attacked and would be defeated.

The Five-Year Plans set targets for production, involving the whole of the Soviet Union. Posters, promoting collectivisation and industrialisation, were created to persuade people everywhere that they were part of a shared plan to build a better society.

★ **FIVE-YEAR PLAN**

This propaganda poster reads:
'*With faster tempo in full-swing. The Five-Year Plan in Four!*'

Stalin claimed: '*there are no fortresses the Bolsheviks cannot storm!*'

When Five-Year Plans were completed, by people working 12-hour days, often to exhaustion or even death, he said:

'*The pace must not be slackened! On the contrary we must quicken it ...*'

New posters appeared proclaiming: '*The Five Year Plan in Four*'.

INDUSTRIALISATION

The first Five-Year Plan (1929-32) targeted industrialisation, investing in heavy industry in underdeveloped parts of the country. Workers were forced to go to settlements in far-flung areas, uprooting whole families and groups of people.

The Soviet Union itself was at risk. Therefore, personal needs were irrelevant. More than fifteen million peasants were moved off the land to become workers in towns. There was heavy punishment for anyone taking days off or slacking; to complain was to betray the country.

COLLECTIVISATION

To raise the money for industry, surplus food was needed to sell abroad. But there was no surplus food. To increase production, Stalin introduced a policy of collectivisation. Peasants and farmers would no longer be able to farm for themselves. Fifty to 100 holdings would be grouped together in a unit and, *'to squeeze out all capitalist elements from the land'*, farmers would work together and be paid at prices determined by the State.

Collectivisation forced peasants to sell their goods to the State at low prices, but they were unwilling to do this. Millions of kulaks – regarded as exploiters, but often just hard-working and efficient farmers – were deported to far-flung places, or fled to the towns. The initial upheaval disrupted food production and contributed to the famine of 1932-33, during which millions of people died.

By the end of the 1930s it is believed that over ten million peasants had left the countryside for the towns, causing food shortages, rationing and overcrowding.

A WORLD POWER

While men and women worked extremely long hours for very low wages, opening mines and building industrial plants in distant corners of the country, in the cities, monumental buildings were built to prove to the world that the USSR was now a world power.

Stalin announced: *'Life has become better, life has become gayer!'*

Yet for most people life remained dull with a complete lack of choice in all products. Consumer goods were hard to find or unobtainable. Clothes were utilitarian and without style and all objects, from shoes to sofas to tinned foods, looked the same and were packaged in exactly the same way. In many cafes and restaurants, plates and cutlery were in such short supply that people had to queue up for these as well as for the food.

IN THEIR OWN WORDS

We are advancing full steam ahead along the path of industrialisation – to socialism, leaving behind the age-long Russian backwardness. We are becoming a country of metal, a country of automobiles, a country of tractors.

Joseph Stalin, 1929

WORKERS ★
A poster advertising
International Workers' Day.

THE GREAT PURGES

During Stalin's long reign in office he constantly felt surrounded by enemies. Japan and Germany posed a real threat, but Stalin felt that people close to him could betray him at any time. His paranoia made him especially fearful of those Bolsheviks who had taken part in the Revolution and might disagree with his policies.

SHOW TRIALS AND SURVEILLANCE

Many engineers and other professionals, known as '*bourgeois specialists*', were made to sign false confessions in a series of arrests and show trials, which began in 1928. Then, between 1934 and 1939, Stalin organised a massive purge, known as the 'Great Purge' or the 'Terror'.

Major figures in the Communist Party and the government, and many Red Army high commanders were killed after being convicted of treason in show trials, where they were forced to confess to all sorts of unlikely and ridiculous crimes. Millions of so-called '*enemies of the working class*' were imprisoned, exiled or executed.

The purges were organised by Nikolai Yezhov, aided by widespread police surveillance, suspicion of 'saboteurs', imprisonment and executions. The Cheka changed its name to NKVD (State Secret Police), which later became the KGB.

IN THEIR OWN WORDS

The prisoners were charged with every possible crime, including high treason, murder, spying and all sorts of sabotage. They were accused of plotting to wreck industry and agriculture, to assassinate Stalin and break up the Soviet Union ...

Fitzroy Maclean
(British Diplomat)

★ **STALIN AND YEZHOV**
Nikolai Yezhov (right) was responsible for Party discipline and organised the purges for Stalin (centre).

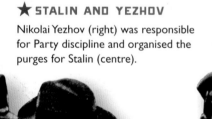

★ **LABOUR CAMP**
Fierce, sadistic NKVD officials ran the huge network of forced labour camps.

★ **LABOUR CAMP**
Thousands died in these (now abandoned)
labour camps in Siberia and the Arctic.

GULAGS

Gulags – labour camps – were set up in Siberia
and the Arctic, and prisoners were forced
to do hard manual work on mining projects
and construction sites. They lived in totally
inadequate conditions, had little food and were
badly treated by the secret police who ran the
camps. Millions died from cold and starvation.

★ **GULAG INMATES**
Back-breaking work filled the long days
of the Gulag inmates, known as *zeks*.

Although almost impossible to produce a realistic
figure, KGB files indicate that between 1928–52
over 20 million Soviet citizens died due to forced
collectivisation and purges. Almost every family in the
USSR lost at least one person as a victim of this period.

Many professionals and former Bolsheviks fled abroad. But even
those living abroad were not safe and Trotsky, in exile in Mexico,
was killed by undercover Soviet agents.

A side effect of this forced elimination of skilled people was that
it enabled others from poor, working-class backgrounds to move
into the new social hierarchy and become successful, as was the case
with future leaders Nikita Khrushchev and Leonid Brezhnev.

REPUBLICS OF THE USSR

The USSR, as its name implies, was made up of many different republics and nationalities. The majority (60 per cent) were Slavs – Russians, Ukrainians and Belorussians – and the dominant culture was European Russian. But just as there is a world of difference between the Arctic tundra of the north and the abundant vegetation of the warm south, so people from the different areas of the USSR had very different experiences and needs.

A BETTER LIFE
– BUT WITH PROBLEMS

In the 1920s, the Soviet government encouraged national identity and non-Russian peoples were allotted autonomous republics. Even the Jews, traditionally the target of anti-Semitic pogroms, were given their own autonomous republic – Birobidzan. Under a policy known as *korenizatsiia*, education in the republics was provided in native languages, and help was given to

develop local administration and culture. National literacy increased and many dance and theatre companies thrived. But there were also problems. Dominant Russians in the republics, whom Lenin labelled 'chauvinists', had many of their privileges removed and were often discriminated against with regard to housing, education and employment.

STALIN'S REVERSAL

Stalin, who was Georgian himself, was not opposed to the principle of self-determination for the nationalities, but in practice he undermined this by rigidly centralising all policies. For example, under *Gosplan* – State planning – the republics' economies had to be developed, not to suit their own needs, but for those of the Soviet Union as a whole. Uzbekistan, for example, was made to concentrate on cotton production, even though its prime minister complained: '*We cannot eat cotton*'.

Stalin's emphasis on the Russian identity of the USSR downplayed the other nationalities and increased the Russian chauvinism that Lenin had wanted to end. The introduction of internal passports in 1930, listing nationality and preventing people from moving from one town to another without police permission, meant that non-Russians could easily be identified and discriminated against.

In 1939-40, when Estonia, Latvia, Lithuania, West Belorussia and West Ukraine became part of the Soviet Union, most of their army officers and professional people were either murdered or deported to Kazakhstan or Siberia. When Russians replaced them in key positions, tensions grew in the national populations.

The Soviet Constitution promised much to the non-Russian nationalities, but in reality they had little freedom or opportunity. A feeling of resentment and hostility towards Russia and communism smouldered beneath the surface of everyday life – hostility that would eventually erupt.

★ **COTTON PICKER**
The cotton picker smiles as she works, but in Uzbekistan, cotton was produced at the expense of food.

★ **NATIONALITIES POSTER**
The different nationalities join together to work for the USSR.

★ EDUCATION

Soviet society aimed to turn an illiterate nation into a land of readers, creating a highly disciplined educational policy, which encouraged the skilled and talented.

EDUCATIONAL POLICY

Schools were co-educational and comprehensive. All pupils studied the same curriculum from the same textbooks six days a week. There were boarding schools for disabled children and also for gifted children, specialising in art, music, ballet, science and sport.

Children across the USSR studied in their native language – Georgian, Ukrainian, Armenian and so on. They also learnt to read and write in Russian.

At the age of 15, young people went to technical college for three to four years to learn a trade, nursing or clerical work. Or they went to general school for two years before going to university or out to work. Many peasants, workers and young communists were sent to higher education in technological institutes and engineering schools.

In the late 1920s, when Stalin wanted to replace the old 'bourgeois intelligentsia' with a new Soviet 'workers' and peasants' intelligentsia', manual labour – farm or factory work – was taught in schools.

★ OCTOBER

Books were very cheap and stories about Red October were in every school.

★ ADULT EDUCATION

Adult education played a huge part in Soviet planning.

THE CURRICULUM

By the 1930s, when a new elite of highly skilled and educated people was needed, manual labour was replaced by a more traditional curriculum with regular tests and examinations, together with the study of Marxism-Leninism ideology.

Schools were places where socialist values could be reinforced. Work charts and achievements were displayed on walls and there were school councils and school monitors. Under Stalin, it was their duty to report on any teachers or students with 'anti-Soviet' views.

Schools were built all over the USSR from the Ukraine to Uzbekistan. In 1897, 40 per cent of males aged between nine and forty-nine could read or write. In 1939, this had risen to 94 per cent.

PIONEERS

After school, children aged ten and over went to 'Pioneer Palaces', where they could practise woodwork, folk dancing, photography and sport. Many went to Pioneer camp for a month in the summer.

Aged 15 and over, they joined the *Komsomol* (Communist Youth League), training to become activists in the Party, carrying out Party activities, which included exposing any abuse of officialdom.

NOMENKLATURA

By the late 1930s, a new elite of teachers, scientists, skilled workers and managers had emerged. These people received higher wages and benefits, including better housing and access to foods that were scarce. These privileged Party members became known as the *nomenklatura*.

★ COMMUNIST YOUTH

In this Ukrainian poster, Pioneers dressed in white and red swear an oath *'to stand firm for our Communist Party'*.

★ FAMILY AND ARCHITECTURE

IN THEIR OWN WORDS

The room had no running water; sheets or curtains marked off subareas where two or three generations slept and sat; food dangled out of winter windows in sacks. Shared sinks, toilets, washtubs, and cooking facilities … lay either in a no-man's land between the dwelling rooms or down an unheated, laundry-festooned hallway.

Anonymous, 1930s

The redistribution of housing after the Revolution caused the destruction and disfigurement of many beautiful buildings, as palaces and mansions were turned into communal homes. Ceilings were damaged when partitions were built in former salons and ballrooms to create living spaces for the many, rather than the few.

BUILDING A NEW WORLD

Wealthy people were forced to share their homes with the poor, partly in a war against wealth but also in an attempt to bring about a different, collective way of life. This put into practice the basic idea of communism — that the individual would become totally engaged in the community.

Soviet architecture aimed to move people away from the private 'bourgeois' living of the past. In the 1920s, the Constructivists in the Union of Contemporary Architects wanted to build communes, where everything would belong to everyone — even clothes and underwear. Cooking and cleaning would be carried out by all; women would sleep in one big bedroom and men in another, with private rooms for sex.

The building that came closest to this ideal was the Ministry of Finance house — Narkomfin — in Moscow (1928-30). It had shared laundries, bathrooms, kitchens, dining rooms, nurseries and schools — but also private living spaces.

★ COMMUNAL LIVING
Families shared the kitchen in communal appartments.

Lavish and imposing public buildings, such as grandiose Moscow University, were built to impress the world and Soviet citizens alike.

LIVING SPACE

All houses and apartments in towns and cities were owned by the State, and local housing authorities decided how much space each citizen could have. In 1930s Moscow, average living space per person was 5.5 square metres. Councils had the power to evict residents and move new residents into apartments that were already occupied. Most people lived in tall apartment buildings with one family per room, and the kitchen and bathroom shared with other families. Apartment blocks were often run by committees elected by the inhabitants, with heating supplied and controlled by communal boilers. Rents were very low and there were few or no costs, but there could be many restrictions.

If a couple divorced or had more children it was very difficult to move house; this caused overcrowding and domestic violence. However, children tended to enjoy communal living as there were always other children to play with.

From 1932, when many peasant farmers flooded into the towns to work, official residence permits were issued by the security police, leading to the growth of a housing black market — illegal buying and selling of living space.

ЗА СОЦИАЛИСТИЧЕСКУЮ КУЗНИЦУ ЗДОРОВЬЯ

ЗА ПРОЛЕТАРСКИЙ ПАРК КУЛЬТУРЫ И ОТДЫХА

★ GORKY PARK

Most large towns had a theatre and a park. The Central Park of Rest and Culture, stretching almost 3 km along the banks of the Moscow River, was named after the writer, Maxim Gorky.

THE SECOND WORLD WAR

Fear of attack was always present in the Soviet Union. In August 1939, after failing to conclude anti-Hitler pacts with other European powers, Stalin entered into a non-aggression pact with Adolf Hitler's Nazi Germany. Hitler had always wanted to expand eastwards into Russia, and in 1941 he violated the agreement and attacked the USSR.

Stalin joined with Britain and the USA to fight Nazism, but during the Great Purges, many army officers had been removed from power, leaving the Russian military very weak. At first, the Germans seemed to be winning. They destroyed 20,000 Soviet tanks and took more than two million Soviet prisoners.

THE TIDE TURNS

Extremely icy, wet weather and relentless Soviet resistance outside Moscow and Leningrad (formerly Petrograd) gradually drove back the Germans. Roads turned to mud, and German vehicles and soldiers froze in icy temperatures of -35°C.

Stalin changed army leaders several times. He encouraged partisans to blow up bridges and railways, and destroy crops and factories to prevent the Germans receiving

IN THEIR OWN WORDS

> The issue is one of life and death for the peoples of the USSR. We must mobilise ourselves and reorganise all our work on a new wartime footing, where there can be no mercy to the enemy.
>
> Joseph Stalin,
> July 1941, radio broadcast

ВОИН, ОТВЕТЬ РОДИНЕ ПОБЕДОЙ !

★ **MOTHER RUSSIA**
This 1942 poster shows how the battle became one for 'Communism and Mother Russia'. It reads: 'Soldier, answer the Motherland with victory!'

supplies. He motivated people to fight, claiming the battle was not for communism alone but for '*Communism and Mother Russia*'.

Stalin also turned to the priests for help, asking them to say prayers for victory and to raise money for tanks. He restored the Patriarchate, which the Bolsheviks had abolished in 1925.

SIEGE AND SUFFERING

Leningrad suffered 900 days of siege. Three million people were trapped in the city and over 900,000 died. There was no transport, fuel or light. Anything edible was eaten, including human corpses. Soup was made from boiled book-bindings.

In 1942-3 over one million Soviet troops died. Yet despite heavy losses, the Red Army managed to defeat the Germans at the decisive Battle of Stalingrad. Soviet soldiers put up such ferocious resistance that, after months of fighting, the Germans surrendered. The Red Army brought the war in Europe to an end by capturing the German capital, Berlin, in May 1945.

During the four-year war, 25 million Soviet people died, but Stalin's reputation as a leader grew. The USSR came out of the war as a superpower alongside the USA.

Stalin said:

'*We have survived the hardest of all wars ever experienced in the history of our Motherland ... the Soviet social system has proved to be more capable of life and more stable than a non-Soviet system.*'

★ **STALINGRAD**
Relentless fighting led to the defeat of the Germans at the decisive Battle of Stalingrad (1942–43).

★ **BERLIN, MAY 1945**
Soldiers raise the Soviet flag over Berlin to mark the end of war in Europe.

47

THE COLD WAR

Stalin always had a deep fear of western invasion and subversion. After the Great Patriotic War, tensions developed between East and West. The West feared that the spread of communist influence would destroy the capitalist economy and values. The Soviet Union feared that the West wanted to control and destroy the USSR. In 1949 the USA formed a military alliance with some Western European countries under NATO (North Atlantic Treaty Organization).

USSR

GDR POLAND
CZECHOSLOVAKIA
HUNGARY
ROMANIA
BULGARIA
ALBANIA

★ **WARSAW PACT**
The countries of the Eastern bloc that entered into the Warsaw Pact.

★ **FORMER ALLIES**
From left to right: Churchill, Roosevelt and Stalin – often known as the 'Big Three' – became uneasy allies after the war.

IRON CURTAIN

To defend against any NATO aggression, Stalin placed Soviet forces in the countries the USSR had liberated from German occupation in the Second World War, creating the 'Eastern bloc'. In 1955 the USSR set up an alliance with other East European countries in the Warsaw Pact.

When Stalin imposed communist leaders on neighbouring countries, including Czechoslovakia, Poland and Hungary, hostilities between the capitalist countries and the Eastern bloc grew into what became known as the Cold War, a time of tense division between East and West that lasted 45 years.

Built in 1961, the wall became a concrete symbol of the Iron Curtain.

In 1946 British Prime Minister Winston Churchill referred to this division, saying:

'... an iron curtain has descended across the continent ...'

BERLIN WALL

Following the war, Germany was divided into four zones, administered by the USSR, Britain, the USA and France. The capital Berlin was also divided between these countries. When the three parts of the city occupied by the Western Allies joined together to become West Berlin, it became a small, isolated area surrounded by the East. East Berliners began to flee to the capitalist West, until communists built the Berlin Wall to stop them.

NUCLEAR WEAPONS

During the Cold War, both sides developed sufficient nuclear weapons to destroy each other and many more countries, in a dangerous and expensive arms race.

This, together with the cost of the military and maintaining control of the satellite countries, took up most of the Soviet economy — at the expense of consumer goods.

⭐ CHECKPOINT CHARLIE

Checkpoint Charlie was the name given to the famous crossing point in the American sector of the Berlin Wall.

★ WRITERS AND ARTISTS

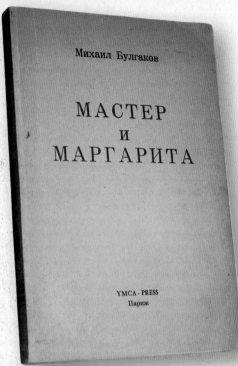

★ THE MASTER AND MARGARITA

Mikhail Bulgakov's famous novel, which criticised Soviet society, was not published until 1967, twenty-six years after his death.

★ SOLZHENITSYN

This was the first novel to reveal what was happening in Stalin's Gulags.

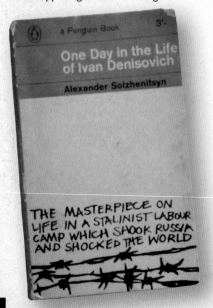

Stalin saw the artist as *'the engineer of the human soul'*, but he also feared their powerful influence.

CENSORS

His 'reign of terror' soon turned from *'bourgeois managers of industry'* to *'bourgeois'* specialists in the arts. He decreed that all creative works of literature had to be passed by the Union of Soviet Writers and needed to conform to the rules of 'Socialist Realism'.

This meant all works had to be written in a realistic and simple way that was easily understood by everyone. They had to praise communism and spread uplifting messages, with no mention of hardship.

Those who conformed were given privileges: better apartments, access to special health clinics and holiday homes. Those who didn't conform had their works banned, could be imprisoned, exiled or tried and sent to Siberian and Arctic labour camps. Writers read their works to one another in secret, fearing that they wouldn't pass the censor.

Arrests took place in the early hours of morning. The sound of a car drawing up, feet pounding up the stairs, followed by loud knocks heralded the inevitable. Many had already packed a bag to take with them when they were arrested.

WRITERS

Maxim Gorky conformed and became head of the Union of Soviet Writers in 1934-36, where he did his best to protect fellow writers from persecution.

Boris Pasternak's epic novel about the Revolution, *Dr Zhivago* (1957), won the Nobel Prize for Literature, but was banned in the USSR. He was forced to refuse the prize and expelled from the Union of Soviet Writers.

Alexander Solzhenitsyn, arrested for 'malicious slander' for anti-Stalin remarks, was sentenced without trial to eight years in the Gulag. In 1962, he published *One Day in the Life of Ivan Denisovich*, exposing life in a Stalin prison camp. In 1974, he was exiled to the West, where he made known the truth about the Gulags.

Many writers went underground, producing *samizdat* — self-published uncensored writings that were handed round and read in secret — or singing ballads, like writer and musician, Bulat Okudzhava.

POETS AND PAINTERS

Poet Osip Mandelstam, sentenced to five years for 'counter-revolutionary' activities for writing a satirical poem about Stalin and reading it to his friends, was sent to the Arctic labour camps, where he died in 1938.

Poet Anna Akhmatova felt it was her duty to be '*the voice of memory*'. After spending hours in line with other women outside the prison where her husband and son were held in the 1930s, she promised '*the truth will be told and I shall tell it*', which she did in *Requiem* (1963).

Art also had to conform to Socialist Realism, depicting heroes of the Revolution or celebrations of happy workers.

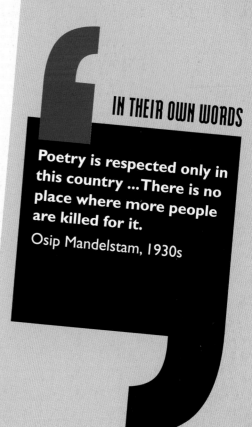

★ **HAPPY WORKERS**

Just graduated, we are going into a new life,
Akhmed Ibadullovich Kitaev, 1953.

★ STALIN'S FUNERAL

Thousands mourn the loss of Stalin, many carrying icons of their '*Father leader*'.

IN THEIR OWN WORDS

> I'll never forget going to see Stalin's coffin. The crowd turned into a monstrous whirlpool. I was walking but was carried along by the crowd. I was saved by my height. Smaller people were smothered alive. People howled – "Get the trucks out of the way!"
>
> Yevgeny Yevtushenko

KHRUSHCHEV

Stalin died in 1953 and was laid in state in Moscow's Red Square. Thousands queued to see him, many in tears at the loss of their '*Father leader*'.

Stalin's eventual successor, Nikita Khrushchev, began a process of 'de-Stalinisation', during a period that became known as 'the Thaw'. This involved a re-examination of Stalin's rule and an attack on Stalin's cult of personality. About eight million political prisoners were released from the Gulags, and many of those who had been killed under Stalin's rule were declared innocent.

THE THAW

Khrushchev set about improving the livelihood of Russian citizens, 'humanising' the Soviet system and increasing the production of consumer goods. His Virgin Lands scheme created new grain-growing areas in Siberia and Kazakhstan.

In this period of freedom, poetry was hugely popular and poets Andrei Voznesensky and Yevgeny Yevtushenko, became like 'pop stars'; their poetry readings filled whole football stadiums.

KHRUSHCHEV ★

Khruschev inspects wheat growing in the fields of his Virgin Lands scheme.

A NEW PROGRAMME

In 1961, a new Communist Party Programme (the third of its kind) by Khrushchev promised that over the next 20 years:

'... housing, public transport, water, gas and heating will become rent-free for all citizens. There will be free medical services, free use of sanatoria and free medicines. The transition to free meals at factories and collective farms will begin ... the Soviet people will have the highest standard of living in the world.'

The Soviet economy did become the second largest in the world, after the USA, although not the second most prosperous. In the first five years of the seventies the number of private cars doubled to 3.6 million. Many people had televisions, sewing machines, washing machines and refrigerators for the first time.

THE CUBAN MISSILE CRISIS

But in 1962 Khrushchev's foreign policy almost caused a Third World War, when he decided to base nuclear weapons on Cuba, a communist island off the coast of the USA. The missiles were being transferred across the ocean by ship when, at the last moment, Khrushchev gave orders for them to be withdrawn and returned to base, following a US pledge that it would not try to invade Cuba again.

⭐ **CRISIS**
Alarmed Americans crave news about an imminent nuclear 'Red' attack during the Cuban Missile Crisis.

⭐ **NUCLEAR MISSILES**
Missiles leave the USSR for Cuba, heading towards a potential Third World War.

★ LEADING THE WORLD

In space technology and sport, the Soviet Union became a world leader. Its superior scientific research and technology culminated in the launch of the first space satellite – *Sputnik 1* – in 1957.

THE SPACE RACE

Sputnik I was followed by a range of pioneering space events:

The dog, Laika, ventured into space in *Sputnik II*, to coincide with the fortieth anniversary of the October Revolution.

In 1961 Yuri Gagarin completed an entire orbit of Earth in the first manned space flight in *Vostok 1*.

In 1963 Valentina Tereshkova became the first woman in space, reinforcing Russia's policy of 'equality for women'.

The State made science a top priority and Khrushchev made the most of this, often holding public receptions for cosmonauts when they returned to Earth.

IN THEIR OWN WORDS

Arrogant commentators told us that Russians with their bast (birch bark) shoes and footcloths would never be a great power. But once-illiterate Russia has pioneered the path into space.

Nikita Khrushchev, April 1961

★ SPACE

This poster portrays a triumphant Russia conquering space.

COSMONAUT ★

Yuri Gagarin became an overnight star, following his orbit of Earth in *Vostok I*.

Наш триумф в космо
гимн Стране Совето

AEROFLOT

State-owned Aeroflot became the largest airline in
the world, with a fleet of over 15,000 aeroplanes, flying to
and from about 8,000 international and national airports.
Its helicopters flew to isolated communities, touching down
in the frozen fields of Siberia. In the 1970s, air tickets were
so cheap that some people flew into Moscow to do
their shopping.

SPORT

The USSR also placed a high value on sport,
believing that physical accomplishment
made for healthy, contented citizens. Every
town had a park, and all cities had well-
funded sports clubs. There were over 50
sports boarding schools and young people
everywhere were encouraged to join the
Komsomol youth movement.

Sport brought international prestige and
displayed the success of the USSR, which
won many Olympic titles. National
teams were set up for football, gymnastics
and athletics. Those with talent could
receive State privileges right up until the
age of retirement.

BALLET

In ballet, too, international acclaim was received by
the Bolshoi and Kirov ballet companies as they toured
the world. But some performers, including Rudolph
Nureyev and Mikhail Baryshnikov, experiencing the
freedoms of the West and realising the limitations of
Soviet society, defected.

★ OLGA KORBUT

Known as the 'Sparrow from Minsk',
the Belarusian gymnast won four gold
and two silver medals at the Olympic
Games in 1972 and 1976.

AFTER KHRUSHCHEV

The brief freedoms allowed by Khrushchev were followed by further repression, when Leonid Brezhnev came to power in 1977 and a devastating nine-year war in Afghanistan began in 1979.

AID TO MARXISTS

Oil production doubled in the 1970s and, by selling it abroad, the Soviet Union was able to continue its policy of communist expansion, sending aid to help Marxist revolutionaries in Africa, Asia and the Middle East. It also kept level with the USA in the arms race. But at home, life was deteriorating: there were long queues in the shops and shortages of meat and dairy products, as the collective farms failed to produce enough food.

GORBACHEV

Mikhail Gorbachev came to power in 1985 aware of the need for change. He introduced the doctrine of *glasnost* (openness) and *perestroika* (economic and political reform). He set about de-centralising the economy and allowed free elections to encourage a move towards democracy. He called for:

'A world without violence and wars ... dialogue and cooperation [between nations] for the sake of ... the preservation of civilization.'

★ **AFGHANISTAN, 1979**
Soviet tanks roll into Afghanistan during the Soviet-Afghan War (1979–89).

★ **WORLD LEADERS**
Gorbachev (left), seen here with US President Ronald Reagan, ended the arms race with the West.

For the first time the Russian Republic was given real powers of its own, and Boris Yeltsin was elected as President in June 1991. Soon Lithuania, Latvia and Estonia – always unhappily linked to the Soviet Union – declared their independence and elected their own governments.

GLASNOST

Glasnost brought a relaxation of censorship and the KGB (later the FSB) had its powers reduced and many of its records made public. The Russian Orthodox Church was allowed to publish and do charitable work again, and for the first time western music and ideas were welcomed into the Soviet Union.

Not everyone liked these changes. Leading members of the Communist Party believed Gorbachev was trying to 'westernise' the USSR and destroy the Party. Others, including President Boris Yeltsin, wanted to see more reforms.

A COUP

In 1991 Communist hardliners, including the prime minister and the head of the armed forces, organised a coup against Gorbachev. Huge crowds, led by Yeltsin, gathered in protest. Yeltsin climbed onto a tank and rallied the crowd calling on the army not to take part in the coup. The coup failed.

END OF THE USSR

Following this, the Communist Party of the Soviet Union was abolished. Alienated by the Soviet Union's contradictory nationality policies, many republics declared their independence. On 25 December 1991, Gorbachev resigned. In trying to make things better, he had, in fact, brought the USSR to an end.

The Soviet hammer and sickle, symbols of communism, were removed from the Kremlin tower, and Leningrad reverted to its original name of St Petersburg. In 1992 the Soviet Union became the Commonwealth of Independent States (CIS), a shadowy body, consisting of 12 independent states.

IN THEIR OWN WORDS

Citizens of Russia, the legal president has been removed from power. We are dealing with a right-wing, reactionary, anti-constitutional coup ... It returns us to the Cold War era ... We appeal to all soldiers and servicemen ... to refuse to take part ... We appeal for a general strike throughout the nation.
Boris Yeltsin, 1991

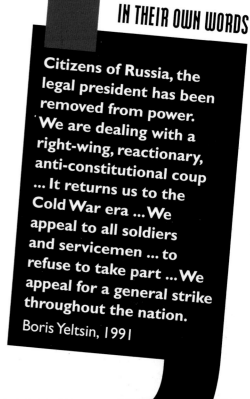

★ YELTSIN

Yeltsin stands on a tank and rallies the crowd to defy the coup in 1991.

AFTER COMMUNISM

With the dissolution of the USSR, Russia plunged into capitalism and the 21st century with typical energy, enthusiasm and chaos.

For the young and ambitious, eager for new experiences, freedoms and the cultural diversity and affluence of the West, it was a time of exciting opportunity.

For the arts there was open discussion in all the mass media, new forms of artistic expression, with street plays performed in the towns and cities, including Moscow's Red Square. The cities of Moscow and Leningrad built modern shopping precincts, attracting top fashion labels, artists and designers from around the world. New music, dance and restaurants filled the streets.

Some exploited the new economic opportunities to the full, buying up assets that had previously belonged to the State, such as oil, gas, iron and steel, to become wealthy oligarchs - among the richest people in the world.

For others, especially the older generation, there was sadness and insecurity at the loss of the certainties that communism had provided, including housing, employment, education, transport and healthcare. In 2000, Vladimir Putin became president of Russia, aiming to strengthen the state and rebuild Russia as a great power.

THE CIS ★

The original 12 countries of the Commonwealth of Independent States. Today, Georgia is no longer a member, and Ukraine and Turkmenistan are now associate states.

★ BAIKONUR COSMODROME

Baikonur Cosmodrome, Kazakhstan is home to the Russian space programme and launch pad to the International Space Station.

ONE HUNDRED YEARS AFTER THE REVOLUTION

Russia is now a very different country from the one it was in 1917. It has changed from an agricultural land to a highly industrial one, an illiterate nation to a literate one, a country where women had few rights to one where most women have independence and equality at work. It survived devastating world wars and was able to defeat Nazism. However, it paid a high price for the changes — with famine, civil war, purges and Gulags.

The rest of the world has also changed. The Russian Revolution was the starting point that led to revolutions in many other countries. The West, fearing the threat of communist influence, developed deadly strategies and nuclear weapons to protect itself.

The Revolution of 1917 was based on a philosophy and a desire for a better society, where there would be equality for all. But the experience of the 20th century revealed that communism in Russia at this time was simply not able to succeed.

The break-up of the Soviet Union in 1991 is still having a significant effect on world politics today.

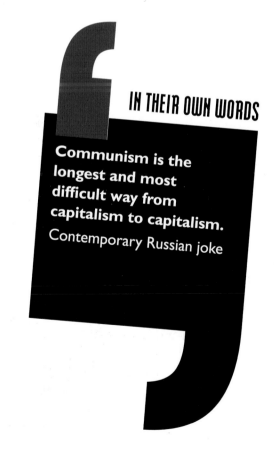

IN THEIR OWN WORDS

Communism is the longest and most difficult way from capitalism to capitalism.
Contemporary Russian joke

TIMELINE/KEY DATES

1848 ★ Publication of *Communist Manifesto* by Marx and Engels

1861 ★ Emancipation of the serfs by Tsar Alexander II

1881 ★ Assassination of Tsar Alexander II

1887 ★ Attempted assassination of Tsar Alexander III

1894 ★ Tsar Nicholas II becomes tsar

1904–5 ★ War with Japan

1905 ★ 'Bloody Sunday': protestors killed in St Petersburg

1906 ★ First Duma (parliament) set up

1914 ★ The First World War begins

1915 ★ Artist Kazimir Malevich launches Suprematism

1916 ★ Rasputin murdered

1917 ★ February revolution leads to abdication of Tsar Nicholas II
       ★ Provisional Government formed
       ★ April: Lenin returns to Russia from exile
       ★ July unrest; Kerensky becomes Prime Minister
       ★ August 'Kornilov affair' – attempted coup
       ★ October Revolution brings Bolsheviks to power

1918 ★ Russia makes peace with Germany
       ★ Tsar Nicholas II and his family murdered
       ★ Civil War between Reds and Whites begins

1921 ★ The Reds win the Civil War
       ★ Famine spreads across the country
       ★ New Economic Policy (NEP) introduced

1922 ★ USSR (Union of Soviet Socialist Republics) formed
       ★ Stalin becomes General Secretary of the Communist Party
       ★ Seizure of church valuables authorised

1924 ★ Lenin dies

1928 ★ First Five-Year Plan and collectivisation of agriculture begins
       ★ First show trial

1929 ★ Trotsky expelled from Soviet Union

1932 ★ Internal passports introduced

1932–4 ★ Major famine spreads across USSR

1934	★ Union of Soviet Writers created and Socialist Realism adopted
1936	★ The purges begin
1938	★ Teaching of Russian in non-Russian schools enforced
1939	★ Nazi-Soviet pact signed between Germany and Russia ★ The Second World War begins
1940	★ Trotsky assassinated in Mexico
1941	★ Germany invades the USSR and the Great Patriotic War begins ★ Siege of Leningrad begins, lasting 900 days
1942–3	★ Decisive Battle of Stalingrad
1945	★ Germany surrenders as Soviet troops take Berlin ★ Creation of the United Nations
1949	★ NATO formed
1953	★ Stalin dies ★ Khrushchev becomes leader
1957	★ Sputnik – first space satellite – launched
1961	★ Yuri Gagarin is first man in space ★ Berlin Wall built to stop East Berliners fleeing to the West ★ Soviet ballet dancer, Rudolph Nureyev defects to the West
1962	★ Cuban missile crisis ★ *One Day in the Life of Ivan Denisovich* by Alexander Solzhenitsyn published, describing the horrors of life in a Stalin prison camp
1963	★ Soviet cosmonaut, Valentina Tereshkova is the first woman in space
1964	★ Leonid Brezhnev succeeds Khrushchev as Soviet leader
1974	★ Solzhenitsyn exiled
1979	★ Soviet invasion of Afghanistan
1988	★ Gorbachev becomes president of USSR, introducing glasnost and perestroika
1989	★ Fall of the Berlin Wall
1990	★ Russian Orthodox Church allowed to practice religion again
1991	★ Yeltsin elected president of Russian Republic in first public ballot ★ Gorbachev resigns ★ USSR dissolved and Commonwealth of Independent States formed
1999	★ Yeltsin resigns
2000	★ Vladimir Putin elected president of Russia

GLOSSARY

Abdicate Give up the throne

Allies Countries supporting one another in war

Amnesty Pardon for political offences

Anti-Semitism Hatred of the Jewish race

Aristocracy The highest and most privileged class in society

Arms race Competition between countries in developing superior weapons

Assassination Killing for political reasons

Austria-Hungary Empire in Central Europe before World War One

Autocracy Absolute rule of one person – the tsar

Autonomy National self-government

Big Three The Soviet Union, USA and Great Britain

Black market Illegal buying and selling of officially controlled products

Bolshevik Russian for 'majority'; a member of the Social Democratic Labour Party, which became the Communist Party in 1918

Bourgeoisie The capitalist middle class; owners of wealth; bosses

Capitalism Economic system where the production and distribution of goods is based on private ownership and profit

Censor An official with the right to ban information from public release

Chauvinism Aggressive patriotism or loyalty to a cause

Cheka Bolshevik secret police (All-Russian Extraordinary Commission for Fighting Counter-Revolution, Sabotage and Speculation)

Civil war War between people of the same country

Collective farm A State-owned co-operative, where peasants shared tools, labour and wages

Collectivisation The enforced joining together of individual farms and land into communal farms, run by committee

Communism Political system where private ownership is abolished and everyone works for the good of society

Conscription The forcing of people to join the army in large numbers

Consumer goods Products used by the people buying them

Cossacks Elite cavalry noted for military skill and horsemanship

Coup Violent or illegal take-over of power

Dandy A man obsessed with style and fashion in his appearance

Democracy Political system where leaders are elected by the people

Dictator Ruler with complete authority over a country

Duma Parliament existing from 1906–17

Eastern bloc USSR and satellites i.e. small countries controlled by the USSR

Elite A select group or class

Emancipation Free from slavery

Exile To be sent away from one's own country and not allowed to return

Gentry Class of people just below the nobility

Glasnost Openness

Gosplan State Planning Authority

Great Patriotic War The Soviet participation in World War Two along various Eastern Fronts

Gulag A vast system of prison and labour camps

Icon Religious painting

Illegitimate A child born to parents who are not married to each other

Industrialisation Development of heavy industry

Intelligentsia Educated and cultured members of society

KGB Secret police; later became the FSB

Komsomol Communist Union of Youth

Kulak Rich peasants, said to exploit others

Leningrad Name given to St Petersburg under Communism; it was also named Petrograd during the First World War

Mutiny Revolt against authority, usually in army or navy

NATO North Atlantic Treaty Organisation: 12 West European countries plus USA and Canada

Nationalise To bring under state control

NKVD State secret police, after the Cheka; later became the KGB

Nazi Member of the right-wing National German Socialist Workers' Party

Nomenklatura Privileged officials who ran the Communist Party

Paranoia Abnormal tendency to suspect and mistrust others

Partisan Civilian fighting the enemy during occupation of their country

Patriarch Head of the Orthodox Church

Patriarchate The official office of the Head of the Orthodox Church

Perestroika Economic and political reform

Pogrom Massacre of Jews, organised by the State

Proletariat People who work for wages; exploited working class

Propaganda Information spread for political purposes

Purge Under Stalin, getting rid of undesirable people

Red Army Soviet army

Red Guards Bolshevik's own armed workers

Requisition Officially seize resources or property

Satellite countries The countries under Soviet control (Czechoslovakia, Poland, Hungary, Bulgaria and Romania)

Samizdat Self-published, uncensored writing

Siberia North-eastern part of Russia

Socialist Realism Art depicting real life that everyone can relate to

Soviet A citizen of the former Soviet Union; also an elected workers' or peasants' council

Soviet Union See USSR

Terror Stalin's purges of the 1930s

Tsar Russian ruler before the Revolution

Tundra Treeless, arctic region

Urban Situated in a town or city

USSR The 15 republics that became part of the Union of Soviet Socialist Republics, which lasted from 1922–91

Warsaw Pact Military alliance of USSR with Albania, Bulgaria, Czechoslovakia, East Germany, Hungary, Poland and Romania (May 1955)

BIBLIOGRAPHY

Russian history is treated at greater length in the titles listed below. Here, too, are some Soviet novels and memoirs.

Anne Applebaum, *Gulag* (Random House, 2003)

Antony Beevor, *Stalingrad* (Penguin Books, 1999)

Jonathan Daly and Leonid Trofimov, *Russia in War and Revolution 1914-1922* (Hackett Publishing Co, 2009)

Orlando Figes, *A People's Tragedy: The Russian Revolution 1891-1924* (Jonathan Cape, 1996)
Natasha's Dance (Penguin Books, 2003)

Sheila Fitzpatrick, *Everyday Stalinism* (OUP, 1999)

Geoffrey Hosking, *Russia and the Russians* (Penguin Books, 2012)
Russian History, A Very Short Introduction (OUP, 2012)

Philip Longworth, *The Cossacks* (Sphere Books, 1971)

Michael Lynch, *Reaction and Revolution* (Hodder Murray, 2005)

Bolshevik and Stalinist Russia (Hodder Murray, 2005)

D. S. Mirsky, *A History of Russian Literature* (Routledge & Kegan Paul, 1964)

Brian Moynahan, *The Russian Century*, (Chatto & Windus, 1994)

Robert Service, *A History of Modern Russia* (Penguin Books, 2003)

Martin Sixsmith, *Russia: a 1,000-year Chronicle of the Wild East*, (BBC Books, 2012)

Steve Waugh, John Wright, *The Russian Revolution and Soviet Union* (Hodder Murray, 2006)

Robert Wallace, *The Rise of Russia*, (Time Life Books, 1967)

Stephen and Tatyana Webber, *World Cultures: Russia* (Hodder Headline, 2004)

SOVIET NOVELS AND MEMOIRS

Mikhail Bulgakov, *The Master and Margarita* (Collins, Harvill, 1988)

Evgenia S. Ginsburg, *Into the Whirlwind* (Collins, 1967)

Maxim Gorky, *Mother* (Foreign Language Publishing House, 1907)

Alexandra Kollontai, *For Love of Worker Bees* (Virago, 1977)

Vyavcheslav Kostikov, *The People and Land of Birobidzan* (Novosti Press, 1979)

Edward Kuznetsov, *Prison Diaries* (Valentine Mitchell, 1975)

Nadezhda Mandelstam, *Hope Against Hope* (Penguin Books, 1975)

Boris Pasternak, *Dr Zhivago* (Harvill Press, 1996)

Victor Serge, *Conquered City* (Writers and Readers Publishing, 1978)

Alexander Solzhenitsyn, *One Day in the life of Ivan Denisovitch* (Penguin, 1963)
The Gulag Archipelago (Harper & Row, 1973)

POETS

Anna Akhmateva, Osip Mandelstam, Vladimir Mayakovsky, Bulat Okudzhava Andrei Voznesensky, Yevgeny Yevtushenko

ACKNOWLEDGEMENTS RE 'IN THEIR OWN WORDS'

p. 6 Michael Lynch, *Reaction and Revolution* (Hodder Murray, 2005)

p. 27, 46 *Bolshevik and Stalinist Russia* (Hodder Murray, 2005)

p. 11, 38, 52 Steve Waugh, John Wright, *The Russian Revolution and Soviet Union* (Hodder Murray, 2006)

p. 12, 13, 16, 18, 21 Jonathan Daly and Leonid Trofimov, *Russia in War and Revolution 1914-1922* (Hackett Publishing Co, 2009)

p. 20, 28 Orlando Figes, *A People's Tragedy: The Russian Revolution 1891-1924* (Jonathan Cape, 1996)

p. 33 *Natasha's Dance* (Penguin Books, 2003)

p. 25 Kollontai, R. Schlesinger, *The Family in the USSR* (Routledge, 1949)

p. 31, 56 Geoffrey Hosking, *Russia and the Russians* (Penguin Books, 2012)

p. 34, 54, 57 Martin Sixsmith, *Russia: a 1,000-year Chronicle of the Wild East* (BBC Books, 2012)

p. 37 *Pravda*, November 1929

p. 44 Sheila Fitzpatrick, *Everyday Stalinism* (OUP, 1999)

p. 50 Nadezhda Mandelstam, *Hope Against Hope* (Penguin Books, 1975)

INDEX